Designing Organizations

Stefan Kühl is professor of sociology at the University of Bielefeld in Germany and works as a consultant for Metaplan, a consulting firm based in Princeton, Hamburg, Shanghai, Singapore, Versailles and Zurich. He studied sociology and history at the University of Bielefeld (Germany), Johns Hopkins University in Baltimore (USA), Université Paris-X-Nanterre (France) and the University of Oxford (UK).

Other Books by Stefan Kühl

Organizations: A Systems Approach
(Routledge 2013)
Ordinary Organizations: Why Normal Men Carried Out the Holocaust
(Polity Press 2016)
When the Monkeys Run the Zoo: The Pitfalls of Flat Hierarchies
(Organizational Dialogue Press 2017)
Sisyphus in Management: The Futile Search for the Optimal Organizational Structure
(Organizational Dialogue Press 2018)
The Rainmaker Effect: Contradictions of the Learning Organization
(Organizational Dialogue Press 2018)

Judith Muster works as a sociologist for the chair of organizational and administrative sociology at the University of Potsdam in Germany. At the same time she is a senior consultant at the consulting firm Metaplan, where she consults companies in logistics, the automotive sector and the media industry in the areas of digital transformation, re-oranization and strategy development. In her research she focusses on the topics of leadership, the limits of organizing, decision-making and digitalization.

To contact us:
Metaplan
101 Wall Street
Princeton, NJ 08540
USA
Phone: +1 609-688-9171
stefankuehl@metaplan.com
www.metaplan.com

Stefan Kühl
Judith Muster

Designing Organizations
A Very Brief Introduction

Organizational Dialogue Press
Princeton, Hamburg, Shanghai, Singapore, Versailles, Zurich

ISBN (Print) 978-1-7323861-0-5
ISBN (EPUB) 978-1-7323861-1-2

Copyright © 2018 by Stefan Kühl, Judith Muster

All rights reserved. No part of this publication may be reproduced or transmitted in any form or by any means, without permission in writing from the author.

Translated by: Andrés Crump
Cover Design: Guido Klütsch
Typesetting: Thomas Auer
Project Management: Tabea Koepp
www.organizationaldialoguepress.com

Contents

Foreword 7

1.
The Organization—What Is It, and How Can It Be Understood?—Introduction 12

1.1 The Structure of Organizations 14
1.2 The Three Sides of an Organization 22
1.3 Structure Matrix for the Analysis of Organizations 33

2.
Beyond an Instrumental-Rational Narrowing in the Design of Organizations 36

2.1 The Dominance of Instrumental-Rational Thinking
in the Conceptualization of Organizational Design 37
2.2 The Function of an Instrumental-Rational Approach
in the Design of an Organization 41
2.3 The Limits of the Instrumental-Rational View
of Organizations 43

3.
How Can Organizational Structures Be Designed?............47

3.1 Observational Latencies—the Starting Point in Design.................48

3.2 Communicational Latency—an Initial Definition 54

3.3 Identification of Mobile and Immobile
Structural Characteristics...59

3.4 On the Production of Variations in the Organization 61

3.5 Promoting Selections..65

4.
On Working with Latencies—Conclusion 68

Bibliography..70

Foreword

This book represents a paradigm shift in organization management. Although the idea of organizations as machines that can be operated and optimized is still predominant in the minds of many managers and consultants, it has suffered a tremendous loss in plausibility over the last decade. Based not only on the results of organizational research, but primarily on the reports from everyday organizational practice, it is possible to recognize that organizations do not function as *trivial machines*, for which it is possible to know with certainty which output will result when using a specific input. And yet, even if referring to organizations as "complex," "nontrivial," or "chaotic" belongs to the current lip service of managers and consultants, the perspective of instrumental rationality on organizations is nonetheless still dominant in the literature for change management in organizations.

In contrast to that literature, we would like to demonstrate what the design of organizations can look like, beyond the *machine model* of understanding organizations. It is the possibilities that lie within the organization itself, and not the supposed "Best Practice" from other companies, that should give rise to changes. We demonstrate that it is much more about the development of an organization's hidden possibilities, which are difficult to communicate, than it is about working out the "core competences" of the organization, which are usually easy to spot. According to the approach presented in this book, *blind spots* (observational latencies) inevitably arise from the formation of structures in organizations. These *blind spots* are not necessarily inaccessible; they can be used for processes of change in organizations through the observation of external parties. The challenge in processes of change lies particularly in that, even when made visible, *blind spots* are not easily communicable in an organization. The response to these taboos (communicational latencies), within a protected environment, can provide interesting material for the design of organizations.

We classify our focus on *blind spots* and taboos under a fundamental understanding of organizations within a framework of systems theory. Therefore, we will begin by defining what is meant by the term "organization" and what its main types of structure are (Chapter 1). Subsequently, we provide an explanation as to why, under the concept of organizational design, an ends-means approach is still dominant when designing organizations, and show where the limits of this approach lie from the point of view of modern organizational research (Chapter 2). Based on the considerations regarding the roles of rationality gaps, *blind spots* and latencies, we provide a detailed description of an alternative approach in the designing of organizations (Chapter 3). Finally, in the conclusion, we discuss the possibilities and the limits of such an alternative (Chapter 4).

The approach for the design of organizations that we present here is based on our long-term experience supporting businesses, public administrations, universities, hospitals and nonprofit organizations. Even though this book is the result of practical work in project management and primarily appeals to practitioners in an organization, we aspire to align our approach with the most current insights of organizational theory—especially the systems-theoretical organizational research.

It is not our intention to conceal the fundamentally different ways of thinking and practical uses of organizational theory on the one hand and the organizational practice on the other. The communication barriers between organizational theory and organizational practice inevitably appear because organizational scientists attempt to uphold their theoretical claims, while organizational practitioners try to concern themselves primarily with the quotidian issues in their organizations. Despite these insurmountable differences, it is our goal to present a practically tested approach in such a way that we don't elicit condescending looks from organizational scientists due to what could be perceived as a narrow understanding of organizations. And yet, even if we focus primarily on practitioners, organizational scientists might still be able to find one or two interesting deviations from the classical view of systems-theory; for instance, in distinguishing the three sides of an organization, the structural matrix and the differentiation between observational and communication latencies.

This book is part of a small series, *Management Compact*, in which we present the essentials of organizational management for practitioners, against the backdrop of modern organizational theory. In addition to this volume, there will be books dealing with the subjects of *Managing Projects, Developing Strategies, Influencing Organizational Culture, Developing Mission Statements*, and *Exploring Markets* that will be released in parallel. In the *Management Compact* book dealing with *Lateral Leading* we illustrate the way power, agreement and trust have an effect when designing an organization. As we have written these books using the same "cast," attentive readers might notice the use of related thought processes and similar formulations between the books. These overlaps are intentional and serve to emphasize the consistency of the underlying construct of ideas and the connections between the different books.

We don't believe in "simplifying" texts for managers and consultants by using bullet points, executive summaries, text-flow diagrams, or even practice exercises. We find that in most cases, such supportive features infantilize readers, as it is implied that they are incapable of extracting the central ideas of the text without assistance. Consequently, in this book—as in all of our other books in the *Management Compact* series—, beyond the sparing inclusion of graphics, we employ only a single element to facilitate reading the text. We have inserted boxes to cite examples that illustrate our thinking; we also use them to highlight links to organizational theory more extensively. Readers who are pressed for time or not interested in these aspects can skip the boxes without losing the general thread of this book.

The principles of organizational theory behind this concept can be found in my book *Organizations: A Systems Approach* (Kühl 2013). Especially the first chapter, which deals with what is meant by the term *organization* and what the structure of organizations consists of, serves as the basis for this book. Readers who are interested in empirical research that deals with the distinctions presented here can find it in the book *Sisyphus in Management: The Futile Search for the Optimal Organizational Structure* (Kühl 2018a, forthcoming).

This book was developed in the framework of the Metaplan qualification program "Leadership and Consulting through Discourse." We would like to thank the various participants of this program throughout the years, not only for repeatedly subjecting the approach presented here to critical examination, but also for contributing the ideas and practical experience they gained in the field, as well as the organizational scientists who have continuously scrutinized Metaplan's work in the field for the last decades.

1. The Organization—What Is It, and How Can It Be Understood?—Introduction

The use of the term "organization" is often rash and arbitrary. We apply the words "organize" or "organization" when describing the creation of an orderly system of operations that are geared to a specific goal. We speak of "organizing" and "organization" when different interdependent actions are assembled "into sensible sequences that generate sensible outcomes" (Weick 1979, 3). Of course, we also speak of the "organization" of a family party, the "organization" of groceries in the black market, or the "organization" of a group of friends' seating arrangement at their regular table at the bar.

In this broad sense of the concept of organization, we organize almost everywhere and almost always: social activists organize their protests; a group of friends organizes game nights; families organize their children's upbringing; armies organize warfare and companies organize the more or less profitable management of their businesses. International laws, playground regulations, instruction manuals or game rules—all of these seem to fall under the umbrella of our definition of the concept of organization. However, this definition of organization is not suitable for in-depth analysis, as we are merely describing some kind of order which is used for the achievement of something. The use of the term has become so vague that it comprises anything which is somehow "structure-like" or "orderly."

To differentiate from this broad usage, a more focused understanding of the concept of organization has established itself—not least because of the education in scientific organizational research. Especially in the organizational research informed by systems-theory, we define "organization" as a particular form of social construct which can be distinguished from other social constructs such as families, groups, movements or networks. There are three characteristics that are specific to organizations. They will be explained in detail in the following.

Organizations can make decisions regarding the inclusion and exclusion of people, and they can define conditions for *membership* which would apply solely to the members. Members are aware that they would have to leave the organization when they openly indicate that they do not comply with the programs of the organization, disregard the communication channels, or do not deem other people in the organization as acceptable communication partners.

Furthermore, organizations establish *goals* with which they align their decisions. Even if the instrumental-rational assumption—still supported in the tradition of Max Weber—that organizations are to be understood in terms of their goals could not establish itself in organizational research, goals still play a significant part in the structuring of organizations. As if wearing blinders, the perspective of organizations focuses on a few seemingly important aspects and blocks out everything else.

Moreover, organizations are characterized by *hierarchies* which determine the relationships of super- and subordination of members. Especially the branch of organizational sociology which focuses on micro-politics has managed to convincingly prove that even members on the lowest rungs can have considerable sources of power at their disposal. However, the bottom line is that compliance to hierarchical orders can be made into conditions for membership, which allows unpopular measures to be established.

1.1 The Structure of Organizations

An outsider who is intensively engaged with large companies, public administrations or associations is often awestruck when—despite all the observed contradictions, uncertainties, chaotic processes and surprises—a more or less remarkable product comes out in the end. When studying the various strategies that are "manually" and "secretly" customized to fit the production planning system at the factory of an automobile corporation, it is indeed astonishing that a considerable number of cars manage to leave the assembly line. And it may be initially puzzling that, all the seemingly chaotic operations at the German Railway Company (Deutsche Bahn) notwithstanding, a considerable percentage of trains, albeit with their occasional delays, still manage to make it to their destinations at the end of the day.

Organizations—in spite of all the chaos—manage to distinguish themselves from other social orders such as meeting up with friends, social movements or religious initiatives in terms of their reliability. These social orders do not exhibit the same degree of predictability as organizations. At Apple or at the Department for Interior Affairs, one generally knows which administrative voices are to be regarded as the official opinion of the complete organization; and which voices are simply expressing a personal stance. In the case of a circle of friends, movements and initiatives this is not as clear. Who is the speaker of the freedom movement? Who is entitled to speak on behalf of a circle of friends?

This depends on the fact that organizations, when compared to other social orders, are able to generate a certain degree of permanence. By way of contrast, a group of barhopping friends, the movement against American intermediate-range ballistic missiles or a youth initiative for sexual abstinence of American teenagers seem to quickly disappear from our screens. Moreover, organizations—as can be seen in the cases of Nokia, the YMCA or the Church of Scientology—manage to carry out radical purpose changes (for instance, from a religious association to a profit-oriented company), without significantly confusing their clientele or members.

Organizations seem to have "tricks" up their sleeves which enable them to make internal communication processes consistent, predictable and controllable, and are therefore able to prevent these internal processes from degenerating into a merely random collection of communications. The terms that are used for these tricks in organizational practice and organizational theory are known as "organizational structure" or "decision premises." They define the fact that decisions are not one-off events, but instead have long-lasting effects on the actions of an organization.

> ### EXAMPLE
>
> **Communicational Limitations in Growing Companies in the Internet Industry**
>
> In the example of growing companies, one can observe the formation of structures in fast motion. When, initially, the total number of members of the company still fit around the kitchen table, everyone seems to be able to communicate with one another. These startups often develop a certain arrogance toward the long-established companies, where, it seems, the right hand usually doesn't know what the left is doing.
>
> However, after the organization has grown to a certain size, more and more time is spent determining who doesn't need to communicate with whom: Who does not need to be informed about certain decisions? Which emails do not have to be sent to everyone? Which meetings don't require everyone to be present? In this way, without the participants even being aware of it, limits in communication are created in the form of established communication channels.
>
> While it was possible to function as an "all-channel-network" at the beginning, and every member was able to communicate with everyone else (or could at least assert the claim to communicate with someone), fixed communication channels are now established. Only so is it possible to obviate the "communicational overkill" of an organization.

Employees are bound to these structures in their roles as members. When an individual joins an organization, it isn't possible for them to simply do whatever they want. The membership in an organization is not "naturally" granted, as it is in the case of being part of a family or a citizen of a state. It depends much more on whether one meets the expectations that the organization has set for their members. The responsibilities, chains of command, control mechanisms, administrative bodies, communication channels and resource allocation must be respected; otherwise sanctions may be imposed by the organization. With the formulation of membership expectations, companies, associations, public administrations and other organizations can ensure that members of the organization carry out actions which are not necessarily based on the member's own motivational structures. As Niklas Luhmann succinctly remarked: "Soldiers march, clerks keep records, and ministers of state govern, whether it pleases them in a certain situation or not" (Luhmann 1975, 12).

The "organizational structures"—known as "decision premises" in systems-theory—look like limitations at first glance (Simon 1957, 34ff.). In organizations, a lot of time and effort are invested in delineating the boundaries of the diverse forms of communication by regulating staff recruitment procedures, employment contracts, work time, division of labor, control mechanisms and job hierarchies. Initially, all of these structures have a stifling effect on the numerous possibilities for communication. Work time regulations limit the times when it is possible to communicate (as well as march, keep records or govern) in an organization. Job hierarchies determine who is allowed to speak to whom. Division of labor determines who is allowed to perform certain tasks and—particularly interesting—who *isn't*.

In organizational research, the distinction between three fundamentally different types of organizational structures (or from a systems-theoretical perspective: three different decision premises) has established itself.

Programs

Programs bundle up criteria on which decisions are based. They establish what one is and isn't allowed to do in an organization. In this respect, programs have the function to make sure someone can be held accountable and apportion blame in the organization in case of errors. If an employee cannot achieve the set goal of a ten percent turnover increase, they may look for excuses, but in the end the organizational structure permits the error to be attributed to that employee.

In organizations there are two essentially different types of programs: conditional programs and goal programs (March and Simon 1958, 164ff.). *Conditional programs* establish what must be done when a certain impulse is perceived in an organization. An employee makes a mistake when they don't take the prescribed steps in reacting to that impulse, and can therefore be held accountable. Conversely, it is the person who developed the program, and not the employee who follows the program correctly, who takes the credit for the results of the work processes. *Goal programs* establish what goals or ends are to be met. Goal programming takes place at the top of an organization when, for instance, the production of bicycles is stated as the goal of the company, or an NGO indicates the proscription of a specific type of landmine. However, for structuring purposes, these goals also apply at the lower levels of the organization. Contrary to conditional programs, the selection of means with goal programs is less restricted: the established goal must be reached—no matter how. Still, it must be said that the selection of means is somewhat bound to certain limits set by the rules of the organization, or by legal regulations. But as a rule of thumb, any mean that is not prohibited by the organization (or even by law) is allowed, as long as it aids in reaching its end.

Communication Channels

The second fundamental type of decision premise consists of the communication channels in an organization. By establishing legitimate contact points and responsibilities, the possibilities of communication are significantly restricted to begin with. A great deal of possible contacts and the effect of various possibly helpful and concerned positions in the process of decision making are forgone; only a small number of legitimized contacts and decision makers are authorized and must be respected by the members of the organization, lest they wish to put their membership in jeopardy.

For the members of an organization, setting up communication channels—as is the case with all other types of structures—has an alleviating function. Individuals who are in charge of making a specific decision can rest assured that their decision will be deemed correct and not questioned within the system. Yet they must also assume responsibility in case of doubt, or might be held accountable for the potential mistakes and negative consequences that may arise from their decisions. This is not only a relief for superiors, but for subordinates as well because they know with whom they are and aren't allowed to speak. Communication channels are also helpful when it comes to cooperation between individuals at the same hierarchical level, as, for example, it is not necessary for a particular department to check the information from another department for consistency or usefulness.

There are a variety of ways to regulate communications. The most prominent method of putting firm communication channels in place is certainly through a *hierarchy*. A further important method of establishing communication channels is *co-signing authority*, which is usually arranged at one hierarchical level: various ministers must come to an agreement before a decree can come into effect, or the heads of departments must countersign work instructions before they are officially announced in the organization. Another increasingly important way to define communications channels is as *project structures*. To this end, members of different departments are assembled to work on a project—in other words, a goal program—over a specific period of time. Hierarchies, co-signing authority and project structures can be combined with one another to produce highly specific forms and networks of communication channels. Depending on the combination of hierarchies, co-signing authority and project structures chosen, there will be corresponding changes in the likelihood of cooperation, competition or conflict in the organization.

Personnel

Whereas it is common practice in organizational science to classify programs and communication channels as organizational structures, the suggestion to view personnel as a third and coequal type of structure is somewhat surprising. The reason personnel has been widely ignored in this context can be traced to a blind spot that has inadvertently found its way into organizational research via classical business economics. Due to its orientation on the classic ends-means model, organizational research in business often views personnel merely as a means to an end, but not as something that presents a structuring element in organizations. This fallacy produces such peculiar word combinations as "Organization and Personnel"—for instance when discussing divisions, institutions or academic departments—, which suggest that, analytically, the personnel is to be understood as something external to the organization.

With the organizational structure concept defined above, it is easy to prove the structural character present in decisions made about personnel. Any observer can arrive at the conclusion that in an organization one does not only make decisions *about* personnel, but that the decisions regarding personnel are also important premises for further decisions in the organization. It makes a difference for future decisions which person occupies the position in charge of the decision. In the same position, legal practitioners will often make different decisions from those an economist would make; they, in turn, will decide differently from sociologists.

Organizations have different options when it comes to turning the personnel adjustment screw. The *hiring process* determines which type of person will make future decisions. Already when redacting job ads, candidate profiles and contract specifications there are heated discussions regarding the qualities—and ultimately the criteria relevant for making decisions in an organization—that a person should possess. The *dismissal* of individuals can be used to signal which kind of decisions are no longer desirable in the future. *Internal transfers* can be made in several directions: upward—in the form of a promotion, or to put someone on ice as a figurehead; downward—in the form of a demotion; or lateral. *Personnel development* represents an attempt to change an individual's behavior, so that while remaining in the same position they will arrive at different decisions in the future.

1.2 The Three Sides of Organizations

In projects meant for the design of organizations one can often recognize that only one side of the organization comes to the foreground. When it comes to formal structures, the classic, expert consulting firms of the world are summoned. It is expected of them to reengineer the formal processes of the organization; to make the organogram "leaner" by dismantling departments or hierarchical levels; or to "redesign" the formal employee structure. Because of the disruptions that often occur in such processes of reorganization, systemic process consultants, trainers or coaches are brought in as "cultural specialists," whose task it is to make sure that the "chemistry"—the informal arrangements beyond all formal guidelines—between employees is restored. When it comes to the display side of the organization, marketing specialists, advertising firms or PR agencies are hired and assigned to rebuild, maintain and, if necessary, repair the public face of the organization.

Indeed, there is hardly any organizational design project today that comes without holistic aspirations. Nowadays, even the classic expert consultant firms offer their clients a "culture program;" the systemic consultants aspire to make competent statements regarding their client's formal structure. And by now, measures for the commercialization of change projects play an integral role in the management of the display side in almost every organization. Yet it is still assumed that these three aspects—the alteration of formal structures, the adaptation of organizational culture and the presentation of the reorganization project—interlock smoothly. However, the fact that the requirements for the three sides of the organization are fundamentally different is often overlooked.

The Formal Side of the Organization— Decided Decision Premises

The core feature of organizations consists of the ability to set conditions for membership. The condition requires one to make a decision regarding one's willingness to accept the organizational structures of expectation. The times in which one is allowed to be present in the organization's premises are specified, as well as what one is allowed to do in this time and which organization members one must pay heed to and which can be ignored. If one is no longer willing to meet these expectations, it won't be possible to remain a member of the organization. Simply put, these disclosed membership conditions are the *formal structure* of the organization.

However, in order to conceive of a particular behavior as a condition of membership, it is necessary to make the organization's requirements for members relatively consistent. It is problematic to prove a social worker guilty of having infringed a rule when a formal regulation enables them to take support measures only if proof of authorization can be presented, while, at the same time, a case of severe neglect demands they use such measures of assistance immediately—without the required proof of authorization. Of course, there are inconsistent rules in organizations; every employee could write a book or two about it. But it is precisely these contradictions in the formal rules that enable members of an organization to alleviate the burden of behavioral expectations, as they allow the members to refer to some rule that serves to justify their actions (Luhmann 1964, 155).

Formal structures are, in a nutshell, the "*decided* decision premises" of an organization. Even if this definition might seem somewhat awkward at first, it offers the advantage of drawing our attention to different aspects at once. This definition sharpens our perception of the various decision premises an organization can use to influence decisions.

The Informal Side of Organizations— Undecided Decision Premises

The world of the organization seems to be a much wilder place than the easily communicable formal structures, or even the facade it presents to nonmembers would suggest. Informal structures—unlike formal structures—cannot be set in stone, as its requirements can either be rejected as inappropriate by a prospective member, or the structures are often not recognized by the organization. And even if they did, they wouldn't always allow them to be officially endorsed. At the same time, general experience has taught us that members also tend to fail when they follow the formal requirements of the organization too closely.

One can identify *informality* as part of the organizational structure if an action which is not contained within the expected formal structure occurs with a certain frequency. A pattern doesn't acquire the status of "informal expectation" until it has surreptitiously found its way into parts of the organization, and is no longer expected of only one single member. And only after the sporadic meeting between colleagues from neighboring departments goes from being an exceptional occurrence to a regular "shortcut channel" for meetings, can we refer to it as an "informal structure."

"Informality" is not to be understood as a one-off improvisation to help one trudge through the jungle of guidelines and specifications, but rather as a network of reliable beaten paths that are regularly taken in an organization. Informal structures are also *decision premises*—requirements that are valid for a multitude of decisions in an organization. They encompass all those expectations in an organization that are *not*—cannot be—formulated in the conditions of membership. What they have in common is that, although no actual decisions are made about these expectations, they still make up a part of the expectations within the organization.

Informality is therefore characterized by both its structurability of expectations and how its structures cannot be traced back to official conditions of membership. "Informality," "underlife" and "culture" represent the undecided decision premises in an organization (Rodríguez Mansilla 1991, 140f.). The underlying concept is simple. Agreements are reached about the way organizations should make decisions in the future; but these decisions are not to be made by a board of directors, a party convention or a pope. They simply find their way in unnoticed and become customary practice.

There are several reasons why informal structures can be functional for an organization; an organization that settles for their employees following the formal guidelines would be lost. Not for nothing is "work-to-rule" one of the most effective forms of strike. Not all expectations in an organization can be elevated to conditions of membership. Moreover, formulating conditions of membership seems to be complicated when it comes to attitudes, positions and thinking styles. In these cases, informal structures tend to step in. There are also expectations in organizations which can, in principle, be formalized, their adherence managed; and yet their formalization in organizations, whether consciously or unconsciously, is forgone. The emergence of this type of informality relates to the fact that organizations are confronted with contradictory challenges which cannot be resolved with decisions on a formal level. Organizations can only have a single "consistently planned, legitimate formal order of expectation" (Luhmann 1964, 155). Consequently, reacting to contradictory preconditions of existence requires a high degree of informality. As, for the purpose of their own preservation, organizations "need plenty of services that cannot be worded as formal expectations" and "assigned as an exclusive task," management has often no option other than to allow—or even promote—illegality (Luhmann 1964, 86). In this case it is more a matter of *undecidable* decision premises as opposed to the ones which are simply *undecided*.

Ultimately, this contributes to the preservation of rules in spite of their rigidity. From time to time, rules have to be broken in order to continue existing as rules (Dalton 1959, 219). Only when members of an organization find a situational balance, whether they do this by upholding the formal structures or by taking an informal path, can organizations attain their quick adaptability (see as example Luhmann 1964, 305; Friedberg 1993, 153).

EXAMPLE

Informal Change from Conditional Programs into Goal Program at a Train Terminal

The loading and unloading of containers, as well as general cargo and spillage at train terminals has undergone a drastic mechanization in the last decades. To ensure the fastest and most consistent processing of trains, the requirements for the technical operation of the transport devices is continuously on the rise.

For this reason, a software which communicates orders to transport vehicles was implemented at a train terminal in southeast Europe. Decisions about the trajectories in the industrial premises, sequence of loading and unloading or the use of additional transport vehicles are no longer made on-site by the terminal workers from the "processing" department. Instead, the complex calculations of the employees in the office building known as the "control central" are now in charge. The new timing devices in the vehicles are supposed to decrease the processing times of trains.

In the future, the "processing" department is not to be assessed solely on productivity, but on the correct execution of the control impulses. As a result of this measure, the scope for decision-making for the workers at the tracks has been significantly reduced. On a screen they receive instructions as to which containers must be transported from the trains to the storing and back, and in which order (conditional program). It wasn't possible anymore for the workers to react to unexpected situation with the trains or to adjust their work process. Optimizations such as the "pre-stowage" of containers located far away from the train or longer processing times for special cargo were rarely planned in by the system. Occurrences unprogrammed in the system such as obstructing objects on the premises or the unforeseeable lining up of containers would always lead to deviations from the planned route. Consequently, productivity sank and processing was delayed.

On the one hand, the established goal programs could no longer be reached in the form of productivity targets, on the other, one was instructed to consistently implement the control impulses in accordance to the conditional program.

Trapped in a conflict of goals, the vehicle operators eventually transformed the formal conditional program into an informal goal program: they bypassed the control system in such a way that they were able to readjust to the necessary adaptability to ensure the swift and smooth processing of trains. Simultaneously, they managed to keep up the appearance of the program's implementation. The additional information on the screens was used to make the coordination of the transport vehicles more efficient. The "control central" was satisfied with the successful implementation of the software. After a short acclimatization period, productivity was on the rise.

The Display Side of the Organization

As an outsider, the first descriptions that one hears from a ministry, a company, a public administration, a university or a hospital often sound somewhat stilted. The process in which organizations attempt to draw a cohesive and convincing picture of themselves with filtered reports, intricate organograms, clearly presented procedures or polished statements could be described as "embellishment." In the deceptiveness of hidden complexities and unresolved conflicts, organizations create a "second reality" (aimed at the outside world) that has very little to do with the actual processes of the organization. Such facades of social structures aren't simply there from the start, they must be built and expanded, regularly maintained of and repaired if needed (Luhmann 1964, 113). The systematically planned construction and expansion of facades is accurately denominated "impression management" in organizational research.

With its facade or public image, an organization conveys the way it wishes to be seen. Through conscious or unconscious replication processes from its members, language rules arise which confer a certain security in the contact with the world outside of the organization. Letterheads, official seals and websites serve as symbols which the organization uses not only to achieve ongoing recognition, but also as an attempt to express something.

As the facade is the display side of an organization, the functionality of it must be sought in the expectations projected onto the organizations from the outside. A primary motive for the construction of facades lies in the contradictory requirements that organizations must handle simultaneously. Consequently, facades possess a protective function: they block an outsider's view, so that organizations are able to prepare decisions undisturbed, conceal potential conflicts from the outside world and keep mistakes and possible embarrassments a secret. Meanwhile, the typical discussions about the best possible ways to deal with a situation take place in the background.

Due solely to the fact that members are in contact with different segments of the organization's environment and occupy various positions within the organization, different and often contrasting perspectives develop. Observations from the outside heighten such tensions even further. Consequently, the environment functions as an amplifier for the internal conflicts. If this happens to go overboard and the external image is not well conceived, the organization will continuously lose its ability to manage their own conflicts.

EXAMPLE

Change Management—Or: The Reorganization of the Reorganization of a Medium-Sized Communication Provider

Reorganizations are often followed by further reorganizations. This is not only described in organizational theory, but also in the experience of many employees who are regularly faced by all the fuss of whatever the "next thing" is. What is perhaps evident at an operational level does not necessarily have to match the well-groomed, official appearance of the company's management which corresponds to the organization's external image.

A mid-level communication provider undertook a thorough restructuring of the operative areas in various locations. The locations were not to function as autonomous units anymore. The headquarters made the decision to delegate the large projects that were spread across the locations to the local units of the organization. All employees of a project that was carried out across several locations were now subordinate to an account manager at the company's headquarters who took over both the technical and the disciplinary leadership of the employees. The account manager (often the former location manager) now lead teams of about 200 employees who, in accordance to their role in the project, were re-assigned—regardless of whether they were based in Cologne, Basel or Vienna. A large-scale campaign carried out by the internal communication department announced the central pillars of the "new—future-proof—organization" with brochures and several large events aimed at both clients and employees.

When, after six months, the new organizational structure had not yet "settled in", it was determined that the organization was still not ready to let go of its "location mentality". A change management named "New-Orga Stabilization" was conceived in order to carry out the transition and accompany the implementation of the new processes. A team consisting of company management, workers' councils, human resources and operational managers made up the steering committee of the consultant-lead change project. In order to find out where the problem lay, they relied on the participation of the employees.

During the first project phase it became clear that, in addition to project assignment, a location structure was necessary to ensure customer wishes could be reacted to promptly. This realization was only partially popular with the steering committee. The company management and workers' councils both promoted the New-Orga and justified it to the employees. The external image had already been restructured in accordance to the New-Orga without it having been implemented within the organization. However, with time, it clearly became a matter of reorganizing the reorganization rather than of the consistent implementation of the New-Orga. To satisfy both the critical voices and the external image of the company management, the project name was changed to "New-Orga Readjustment" in the second project phase.

1.3 Structure Matrix for the Analysis of Organizations

When one attempts to comprehend and design an organization, one must focus on diverse structural aspects. Depending on the projects, different structural aspects can be more or less central. When two organizations merge, the realignment of communication channels becomes a priority. Creating a mission statement is often more about the restructuring of the external image of the organization. The strategy processes of organizations are made up of the work on formal goal programs. Yet even if a specific structural aspect is the main focus, it is essential to keep an eye on the relation between the three sides of the organization and the three structure types.

The structural matrix can be utilized for the analysis of different aspects. The interaction between programs, communication channels and personnel and the different alignments of formal, informal and external sides can already be observed at the organizational unit which is most simple to define: the *position*. The position must be occupied by a person. It is programmed by fixed trigger conditions found in organizational manuals or computer programs (conditional programs) or by targets that are strived for (goal programs). Their contact possibilities are limited by predetermined communication channels. Depending on the assignment description, they focus on working on the display side (e.g. PR positions), the formal side (e.g. compliance positions) or the informal side (e.g. personnel development). But also in departments of organizations, all three structure types and all three sides of the organization interact with one another. They are characterized by personnel and their unique decision-making style, and their work is structured by predetermined goal programs and conditional programs, as well as by their integration in the communication channels of the organization. Depending on the task assignment, they align themselves with the organization based on either formal, informal or external expectations. Even at the level of the *organization* as a whole, the interaction between the structure forms can be observed—for instance, when it is determined that an organization only hires certain "types," that unusual communication channels arise in the organogram after a change or that changes of targets or processes can be observed all across the organization.

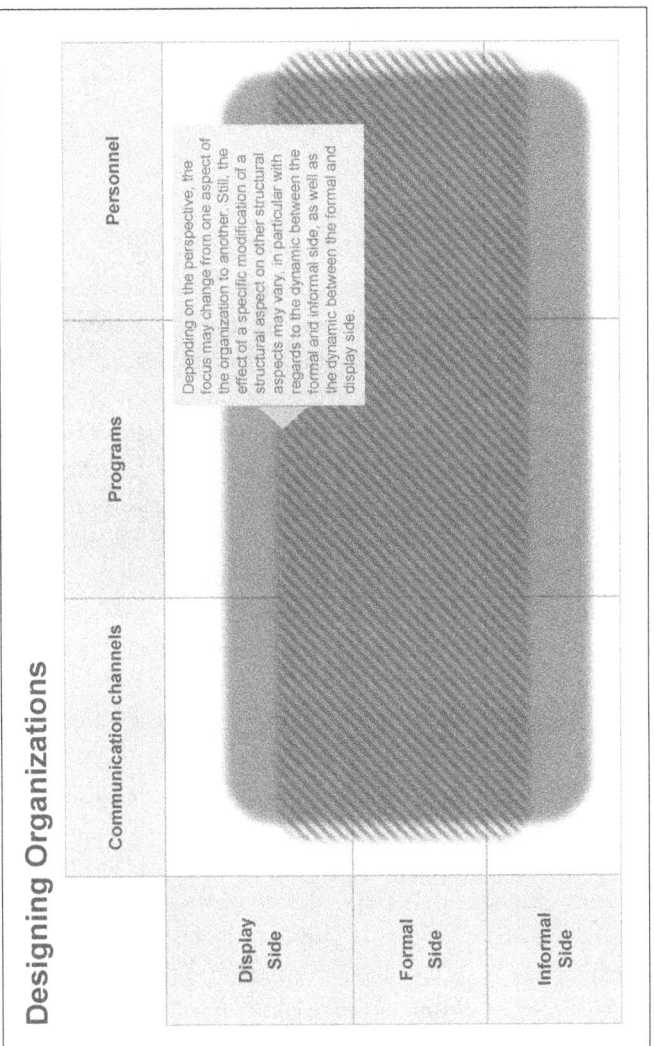

Graphic 1: Structure Matrix for the Analysis of Organizations.

2. Beyond an Instrumental-Rational Narrowing in the Design of Organizations

When one reads reports and descriptions of projects about the change of organizational structures in companies, public administrations, hospitals or schools, they are characterized by a high degree of consistency, conclusiveness and rationality. Regardless of whether it is about a continuous improvement process, the development of a new company strategy or the establishment of a team-oriented structural organization—the success stories are generally dominated by depictions of rationally planned reorganizations. Obstacles, resistance, uncertainties and the unforeseeable are certainly reported on; however, these problems are, as a rule, successfully conquered by those responsible for the process (who are often the same as the authors of the reports) thanks to sudden inspiration, a newly developed tool or a bold intervention. According to the content of the report, in any well planned, flexibly scaled reorganization process, the participants should be able to deal with such challenges.

These rational presentations of change projects (which could already be found in well-known depictions such as the introduction of division structures at Dupont, the introduction of the assembly line at Ford or the development of the Japanese lean management by Toyota boss Ohno) are typical of descriptions which organizations prepare of themselves. Organizations usually see themselves as systems for the making of rational decisions. They distinguish themselves from other systems which make their decisions based on automatisms, traditions or authorities. In rational systems, irrationality, ignorance or forgetfulness can be classified as clear mistakes or as deviating behavior, and can be replaced by more rational decision processes with the appropriate willingness and capability of participants.

2.1 The Dominance of Instrumental-Rational Thinking in the Conceptualization of Organizational Design

Classic organization design processes guarantee the participants a tempting, more rational future. The participants are baited with a "beautiful picture" of the organization, which can be achieved through a rationally planned change process.

Most approaches in organizational design do not differ in that a beautiful picture of a "future reality" is drawn, but rather in *how* that beautiful picture can be achieved. In the case of expert consulting, the consultant grabs the brush and paints the picture which appeals to the client (although not necessarily to all employees). This picture, in the shape of either an expert opinion or a presentation, is ideally so specific and tangible that the client simply must decide to hang the picture on the wall of their office and subsequently restructure the organization according to the picture with the help of the consultant. In the case of an organizational development process, the picture is not painted by the consultant. Rather, it is conveyed to the client that the consultant has the colors and the ability to draw an attractive picture of the company in collaboration with the employees, a picture which they then go on to paint together.

All differences in the execution of the painting process aside, what both approaches have in common is that they work towards an "aesthetization" of the futures of the organization. Oswald Neuberger (Neuberger 1994) described the process in which a picture of the organization is drawn—with filtered reports, organograms or network plans—which has nothing or very little to do with the dynamic, variety and ambiguity in organizations, as aesthetization. In the deceptiveness of hidden complexities and unresolved conflicts, organizations create a "second reality" that has very little to do with the actual internal and external processes of the organization. According to Neuberger, the unspoken longing that managers have to see organizations as consistent and harmonious artwork is present in this so-called aesthetization.

With its reference to its future, the aesthetization in change processes manages to evade the common criticism of the aesthetic picture of the organization not having anything to do with the reality of the organization. Although these aesthetic pictures service the same longing for that consistent and harmonious artwork, they avoid the risk of being accused of creating a discrepancy between the reality and the picture. On the contrary; the discrepancy between the real dynamic, variety and ambiguity of the organization, and the harmonious and conclusive picture of a master plan is more commonly named as a reason for a process of change.

The future is idealized, while at the same time the past is "depreciated." Change projects, change processes and reforms are

Beyond an Instrumental-Rational Narrowing **39**

in this way deficient descriptions, because they are based on the assumption that one can only improve what was before. The past is maligned so that the future can be better. The factual reality is pumped full of counterfactual ideals in order to raise the hope that the organization will one day allow itself to be improved by these guiding ideals and all employees will be convinced by what is "good, important and right."

This discrepancy between the "current-state" and "desired-state" is a main driving force in the classic change process. The energy comes from the master plans, visions and desired states that seem more attractive, simpler and more enlightening than the reality which is perceived as chaotic. It is suggested that, through the consulting process, organizations can achieve a more conclusive, more consistent and eventually more rational functionality, from which all employees would benefit in the end. The energy for change arises from the fact that the intentions of processes of change are hard to refute, as they have not yet been subjected to the "acid test" (Luhmann 2000, 338).

From our point of view, the reason for the complex control and planning conceptualizations dominating a great deal of the change processes lies in this work with the discrepancy between current and desired states. As soon as managers or consultants start to work with aestheticized future designs, they must make use of the fact that they can create a causal connection between reality and future designs. Otherwise, the desired-states would just sit there as a figment without any effectiveness. Managers and consultants must make it clear to companies that recognizing and contributing to the elaboration of solutions is not their sole function. They must claim to possess the tools to unite the flawed organization with the developed ideal conceptualization (Brunsson 1989, 224f.).

Behind this there is a comparatively simple understanding of organizations. As a starting point, a goal is named which will serve as a guiding light for the organizational process. This goal—the argument goes—must be divided into subgoals. Subsequently, the subgoals can be correlated with a position in the hierarchy. In this way, complex end-means chains can be built in which each goal is a mean that allows us to reach a further distant goal, which is in turn only a link in a chain of further goals.

From this perspective, organizations can be described as machines. Organizations reduce their complexity like machines in that they have a clear goal and all means serve this goal. Organizations, like machines, are supposed to work according to a specific plan and cause as little frictional loss as possible. Organizations are a self-contained whole which is made up of precisely defined components. The function of these components is strictly aligned with the function of the machine as a whole. To ensure the complete function, the relationship between these components must be arranged in clear if-then chains.

The aspiration to correlate present descriptions and future designs leads to the "conceptualizations of planned change," "rationalistic views on change management" or to "synoptic planning philosophies." In this case, during the consulting process, it is assumed that the problems of the organization can be identified in the achievement of its goals and consequently strategies are developed which help in reaching those goals. The argument for these strategies must then be conveyed to all employees and implemented in the organization.

2.2 The Function of an Instrumental-Rational Approach in the Design of an Organization

One cannot overlook how attractive the idea of an instrumental-rational procedure in change processes is for management. The "package solutions" promised by such synoptic planning concepts attenuate the anxieties of top management. We explain to all participants that, due to globalization, digitalization and shifting values, they face certain difficulties, but there are operational solutions with which they are able to confront these challenges.

The suggestion is that, in such companies, worked-out master plans for the design of the organization can have an actively motivating effect; master plans help spread a "yes we can" attitude in the organization. A detailed time plan, developed penetration strategies for new markets and efficiency calculations for the future organizational structure suggest a high degree of reality content and convey the feeling to those concerned that the elaborated plans from the organization could be implemented successfully. Subsequently, that can motivate them to take a chance to do something new.

The strategy documents, cut-back suggestions and master plans developed by the organization in collaboration with its employees, or directly conceived by consultants, serve as legitimation for the organization's management. The management of an organization is ensnared in a network of power games and any abrupt cuts would lead to a disturbance in the power arrangements that these power games make up. Master plans for the design of organizations possess the appearance of detachment, objectivity and rationality and are not immediately recognized as trump cards in a new power game.

But this approach has a fundamental problem: changes in organizations don't work according to such instrumental-rational plan conceptions. In the process of such instrumental-rational change projects, it quickly becomes clear how the concept or strategy wears down and loses its appeal. The more specifically a master plan is implemented in reality, the clearer it becomes how similar the contradictions of this concept are to those of all other previous organizational concepts. In other words, the more consistently an aspired goal is implemented in an organization, the clearer the fissures in the goal conception.

To work against the depletion of these master plans and desired states, those responsible, as well as the participating consultants, have a tendency to immunize by personalizing the problems in the change process. When the ideal aesthetic image is not achieved, this is usually attributed to the resistant attitude of employees, middle management's lack of insight or the inability of a specific consultant. A disparity is highlighted between the logical, rational and conclusive plan of the future organization on the one hand, and the irrational, emotional behavior of the employee on the other. In this phase, such explanations as "If only the employees would go along with it …," "Had the consultant not overlooked this aspect …" or "If only the board member had not invested so much energy into other issues …" By attributing the problems and mistakes to people—and therefore seeking the explanations for the problems outside of the system—, the aesthetic, harmonious image of the organization is upheld. Simply put, the plan was good, but the people were not ready for it.

But regardless of how the function of personalization is seen in organizations, their problems tend to be much more fundamental.

2.3 The Limits of the Instrumental-Rational View of Organizations

In order to understand that the ideal conception of a machine-like organization—as depicted by Max Weber—has nothing to do with reality, one doesn't need to be aware of the organizational research which took decades to arrive at this conclusion. Most practitioners already know that reality has very little to do with this simplified instrumental-rational understanding of organizations. The compelling and conclusive self-depictions found in most management books, in the many articles of business journals or in the endless slides at management conferences are in stark contrast with the descriptions of change processes one hears from outside observers: reorganization projects are carried out so that everything can stay the way it was; despite the existing assessment centers, employees are hired because of the well-established networks between university graduates, and not as a result of their aptitude and qualifications; commercial success is attributed to random inventions and sudden market changes, instead of comprehensive scenarios and strategy conferences. Life in organizations appears to be much wilder than the conclusive and rational self-depictions would have us think—and it seems to withdraw itself from the rational master plans of change management.

As James G. March (March 1990, 188f.) pointed out, organizations are continuously and frequently changing, but usually not in the way participants would prefer. Organizations find themselves in a constant, perfunctory, effortless and reactive change process which cannot be steered at will—much to the chagrin of the participants. Organizations react to their environment, but they don't change according to the plans a group of managers and consultants have devised. Sometimes instructions are not followed. Sometimes plans are interpreted and implemented in unintended ways. Only seldomly do organizations actually carry out what they have been assigned to do.

With keywords such as "insecurity," "uncontrollability," "contingency," "limited rationality" and "rationality gaps," we refer to the impossibility of elaborately constructing an organizational meta-goal. According to the convincing findings of decision theory in behavioral science, organizations generally operate on the basis of a multitude of inconsistent and poorly defined preferences (Cohen et al. 1972). For instance, companies cannot solely focus on the target of profit maximization. They have to consider the demands of government policy, unions, consumer associations or environmental initiatives. Seeing that it would be overwhelming for single department to deal with all requirements related to the company's environment, organizations set up different functional areas internally, each of which focuses on the processing of one specific aspect pertaining to the organization's external conditions. The marketing department is the main link to the clients. The public relations department makes sure that the organization is seen in a favorable light with regard to government policy. The legal department takes care of legal issues and it is the job of the department of labor policy to soothe the trade unions.

This is expressed in a variety of dilemmas, contradictions and paradoxes. Organizations need clear goal concepts. However, they also need the readiness to deviate from their set goals if need be. It might make sense for employees to identify with processes, yet at the same time, this identification can hinder the necessary changes. The participation of employees can set free potential for change, but too strong an involvement could negatively affect the organization's focus on dominant goals. While self-organization can be beneficent as solutions are developed from within the organization, outside-organization usually warrants a higher degree of originality. Organizations are faced with the need to create spaces for innovation. However, the creation of these buffers often leads to organizational inefficiency. Organizations rely on learning processes; yet it is precisely these learning processes which are responsible for the decline of organizations. Precisely for this reason, avoiding learning processes can also be a sensible strategy (Kühl 2018b, forthcoming).

As the different requirements must be depicted in the organization, organizations are inevitably created with inconsistent goals and logics. The conflict of whether a production process will be introduced, which could take place between the legal department, research and development and the department of labor policy, is a conflict which inevitably arises in each one of their corresponding functional areas dedicated to the organization's environment. As a result of this focus, while it is true that different requirements pertaining to various organizational environments can be dealt with, the organization is no longer able to carry out a process of rationalization with regard to a single related problem.

All things considered, what would an organizational design which avoids an instrumental-rational narrowing look like?

3. How Can Organizational Structures Be Designed?

Reform projects in organizations are usually rooted in the formal structures of the organization, as these are particularly visible. A new sales structure is to be established in order to tap into a new market segment. A new "communicationally supportive architecture" for the company is to be set up, or a new machine arrangement is planned. The personnel structure is to be changed by hiring additional foreign employees. The procedures in the organization are to be conceived differently, for instance by switching from operating with conditional programs to operating with goal programs.

It makes sense that change projects are guided by formal structures, as these visible structures in an organization are generally well known and easier to mention and discuss. In this way, top management can have a clearer view of how many resources are tied by the project. The line managers obtain answers regarding what is to be changed in the organization. Consultants receive a clearly formulated assignment which allows them to carry out their cost calculations and plan personnel assignment. This results in change processes which are guided by openly visible structures from the very beginning.

This one-sided focus on visible structures doesn't usually become apparent until change projects run into some resistance, unwanted surprises or disturbances. This is for instance the case when an organization has difficulty perceiving changes in its environment, as they lack the necessary sensors because of their structure (for more on this see our *Management Compact Exploring Markets*); or when a thoroughly convincing plan fails because the balance of power between influential figures is at risk of undergoing some changes; or when, even though all participating parties believe in a structural reform, it cannot be carried out because practice shows that the organization works according to completely different rules; or it becomes apparent that a newly developed task distribution system cannot be put into effect on account of "secret game rules." In the following, we present an approach that addresses these blind spots systematically.

3.1 Observational Latencies— the Starting Point in Design

As already shown, organizations, when building structures, have a "trick" at their disposal which allows them to become constant and predictable. With the creation of these structures organizations inevitably develop a highly selective perspective. They develop a sensitivity for something very specific, while developing a distinctive insensitivity for everything else. They observe certain things, but many other things escape their eye. A German automobile company has no interest in agrarian regulations in France (and has no mechanisms to remain routinely informed about them). An internet company has no need to stay on top of developments in the labor market for cleaning personnel, unless they provide virtual cleaning services. A company that does not require shift work will also not set up routines to maintain an awareness of the current studies on the burdens of working the graveyard shift.

These observational latencies are only marginally tied to concrete people; after all, personnel is just one structure type in an organization. Indeed, if a person happens to be promoted to a top-level position, the organization may develop new perspectives, as, comparatively, a top-level position is not as dependent on an organization's communication channels and programs. However, in many cases these blind spots are unavoidable, personnel change notwithstanding. The saying "If Siemens only knew what Siemens knows," which outside observers have said to hint at the hidden potential for innovation of the company, does possess a certain wisdom, as Siemens' blind spots regarding their own potential for innovations remain, for the most part, consistent.

THEORY

Latencies, Blind Spots and Taboos of Social Systems

Whenever practitioners talk and write about latencies, blind spots and taboos, they are referring to the fact that important experiences usually lie in people's subconscious (latencies of consciousness). In this respect, there is an evident link to the tradition of Freudian psychoanalysis. The basic assumption is that people create "defense mechanisms"—such as denial and repression—which contain these blind spots. The blind

> spots are then, and this is the encouraging news, accessible to the therapeutic or consulting specialist, who, in discovering them, can set important impulses for their client.
>
> The systems-theoretical field of sociology—as well as the management and consulting approaches incited by it—is not interested in the latencies found in a person's subconscious. Systems-theory is not there to help us peek into people's minds. This is rather the task of medicine, perception psychology or psychoanalysis. We focus more on the latencies that social systems form on account of their structure.

In observations, latencies—or in other words: blind spots—cannot be avoided. The distinctions used by observers cannot be observed by the observers themselves. They are the observer's blind spot. Or as Niklas Luhmann expressed more fundamentally: "One's own distinction is used as a blind spot which organizes the potential of the observer and can only be replaced in exchange for another blind spot" (Luhmann 2006: 355).

This high degree of selectiveness in observation is functional because it's the only way that social systems can distinguish themselves from their environment. Organizations can only exist because they provide a highly selective view by means of their structures and isolate themselves from the complexities of the world with the blind spots that they themselves maintain. In the attempt to control the design of organizations, it is instrumental to make the hidden alternatives in the organizations systematically more or less visible.

> EXAMPLE

Example of Observational Latencies—
the Embedding of a Consulting Firm

A French consulting firm specialized in ministries and public administrations in developing countries decided to set up a two-year training program for managers and consultants in French-speaking developing countries. The intention of the company was to establish a third mainstay alongside its consulting and assessment business. Although the consultants moved back and forth between the different areas, three different sectors with their respective local rationalities ended up emerging in the frame of the communication channels.

With the company's increasingly expiring—albeit initially undetected—focus on financial performance indicators, it became progressively clearer that no money would be earned with the training program. The stronger cost control became in the company, the more pressure the two employees responsible for the program felt the need to justify the existence of their area of business.

In the framework of a reorganization of the consulting firm, originally organized as a cooperative company, it became obvious for everyone that not only was the program not earning any money for the company, it was in fact losing money. Yet what also became clear in the framework of this reorganization was the fact that the function of the program was not to make money, and three functions, which initially weren't part of the observational focus of the company, gained in importance.

Firstly, the training program had an important acquisitional function. As the consultants of the company would function as advisors in the training programs and consistently brought in their own cases, the managers from the developing countries were able to get to know the mentality and approaches of the consulting company closely. As a result, contacts were made which indirectly led to a series of projects for both the consulting and assessment areas.

Secondly, the training program contributed to the hiring of some of the participants by the French firm. Through the program, close relationships were formed between the trainers and the participants, and the trainers developed a good sense for which participants could perhaps be considered for employment at the consulting company. In the case of projects in the individual countries, the company was able to resort to these former participants as cooperation partners.

Finally, the training program forced the consulting company to explicate their own approaches. In this way, it wasn't only the participants, but also the consultants who were responsible for some parts of the training who learned something from the program. In the framework of the reorganization, it became clear that the central function of the program was not so much to make money, but to pressure the company to agree upon a unifying portrayal of their own approaches.

As a result of concentrating on the profitability of the individual business areas, these functions remained hidden. The reason for this was the shift in focus of the consulting company, which was initially organized as a cooperative company. Although the value of the firm used to depend a lot more on its reputation in the French consulting scene, as well as on the execution of interesting projects, over the years, the revenue generated by the individual consultants gained more and more significance, and recognition was based on the revenue dependent bonuses handed out at the end of the year.

As a measure of recognition, it was agreed upon that the two employees would get a percentage share from both business areas, as long as consulting and assessment projects would result from the training program, new employees would be recruited or publications would be issued. As it proved difficult to attribute the newly acquired projects, new employees and publications to the training program, the program was quickly abandoned. However, thanks to the debate in the company, the benefit of the program eventually became clear.

Observational latency—the fundamental building block of blind spots—is however only one form of latency that we encounter in organizations. Quite often, phenomena—such as existing structures or more obvious structural changes—are visible to almost all participants, yet cannot be mentioned. This missed opportunity can be referred to as communicational latency.

3.2 Communicational Latency—an Initial Definition

Communicational latency refers to the impossibility of addressing certain issues in a given communication. Using a psychoanalytically coined term, we could think of it as a "taboo." In the jargon of managers and consultants, communicational latency is often referred to as a "hidden agenda." Or, to use the complex systems-theoretical formulation, we are dealing with the absence of topics that make communication possible and manageable (Luhmann 1995, 335).

The communicational latency must be maintained by all the participants in a given communication because it has the function to "protect the structures." While it may be true that vanity is a driving factor for giving a talk at an international conference for supervision and coaching, and while this may be apparent to the speaker, this is not something they would openly communicate when asked about their motivations. Regarding the question of one's motivation, one does not simply reply, "Because I'm just vain and want to show that I have more to say about this subject than the other guy." Instead, legitimate reasons are given in such exchanges. For instance: "I was invited to the event;" or "I'm not doing this primarily for myself, but as a favor to others." Subsequently, one would then go on to say a few words about the significance of the topic of the conference (Reemtsma 2008, 407).

It is not always easy to determine which topics of a communicational latency can be openly addressed. An observer, however, will usually have a sense for what topics should not be talked about. It is usually possible to discuss the aspects of the formal structure in an organization—the official communication channels, the created programs and the announced personnel decisions—without any problems. On the other hand, it is not as simple to discuss informal processes pertaining to power, trust and agreement. This can be a problem in as far as organizations may depend on these informal—at times even illegal—structures, but cannot officially include them in a controlled change process due to communicational latencies.

The reason is simple. It can be said that individuals are usually on the safe side when they model their behavior on the rules, as silly as those rules may be. It is enough to simply refer to the established procedure in the company's processes to justify an employee's behavior. When dealing with rules, being "structurally conservative" is still the predominant approach. Niklas Luhmann's idea (Luhmann 1973, 324ff.), which is now considered essential for the design of organizations, states that when an individual digresses from standard procedure, they are not automatically blamed, but rather that the burden of justification is simply redistributed. The digresser is not immediately punished for deviating from that rule; however, they are required to justify why they behaved the way they did (deviating from the rule) and not differently (conforming to the rule) with reference to the system requirements. In the case of these digressions, we are dealing with "structurally critical" approach.

EXAMPLE

Communicational Latencies in a Facility Management Company

Communicational latencies can be observed in the case of the company Technical Facility Management (TFM). TFM is in charge of facility management of the airports nationwide. The facility management activities ranged from simple tasks, such as the replacing of light bulbs, to more complex operations such as the repair of escalators and the maintenance of parking ticket dispensers and computer networks. As an independent subsidiary (albeit entirely owned by the corporation), TFM was outsourced as a result of that popular trend to outsource sections of companies encouraged by consultants.

The facility management company found itself inside a conflicted area delineated by two conflicting goals. On the one hand, the company was tied to a corporation which had a public supply mandate, and as the corporation was solely owned by the state, the facility management company was subjected to restrictive state regulations. On the other hand, in regard to price and quality, the company was supposed to compete with smaller janitorial companies located in the respective cities.

Consequently, teams of craftsmen had to assign orders to subcontractors through similarly complex procedures as applicable to communities and cities, all the while dealing with the pressure of processing customer requirements at a similar speed to independent craftsmen who are not bound to these procurement procedures. It was expected that these teams of craftsmen shut down warehouses with spare parts for the escalators, air conditioning systems or ticket dispensers, and yet at the same time, it was also expected that they were able to repair these machines within a short amount of time, as otherwise, the public interest relevant maintenance of the transportations routes could not be guaranteed.

For this reason, the teams of craftsmen created an array of informal processes. For instance, they had various rooms at their disposal—and this despite the specification from management that the factory and warehouse rooms of the airports were to be reduced. A great deal of the rooms used by the teams of craftsmen were "illegal" and did not show up on any list from the corporation which rented out the rooms or from the facility management company which rented the rooms. Over the decades, the maintenance teams kept "annexing" ventilation rooms, storage spaces under escalators, former rooms for vehicle attendants and utility rooms. These rooms evolved into comfortable individual work stations for the employees, which they sometimes furnished with wallpaper, rugs, microwaves and, in one case, a small picture of Le Pen. Neither the team leaders nor employees were interested in shutting down these "illegal rooms," as no rent had to be paid for them, and they had decentralized storage and work rooms available across the whole complex.

In the individual workshops, unspoken agreements were made between team leaders, consultants and internal organizational developers about which informal aspects could be addressed and which could not. One team clearly signalized their willingness to participate in the active clearing of some of the rooms being used, provided that the fundamental problem of the over twenty occupied, yet not officially registered, rooms was not addressed. In another team, access to the data on the different types of procurement procedures was granted to the consultants, but it was expected of them not to expose the problem of the high percentage of "under-the-table emergency services" in the team.

Especially in the concluding presentations for the upper management, the consultants and the internal organizational developers seemed to actively protect the informal solutions. During a guided tour with the branch manager and a representative of the corporation's headquarters at the end of the workshop, the warehouses were presented in a cleared-up state. The impression was given that the guests were shown all the rooms used by TFM at that particular location. However, in the middle of the tour, a young craftsman in TFM uniform stepped out of one of the illegal rooms and ran straight into the branch manager. Not only did the team leader and the consultant quickly try to escort the craftsman back into the room, but the branch manager went out of his way to overlook the incident as well. At the workshop, maintaining the public image was more important than a discussion about the informal processes for all participants.

How does one concretely proceed in regard to the existing observational and communicational latencies?

3.3 Identification of Mobile and Immobile Structural Characteristics

In spite of all the rhetoric pertaining to the public image of organizations in the style of "Change is our only constant," there are structural characteristics in all organizations which are in fact immobile. Due to a view of the organization's environment ultimately established by the organizational structure, it is considered that there are no alternatives for certain structures—so much so, that it wouldn't be worth it to attempt to change them. Some structural characteristics are so deeply entrenched within the organizational culture that they cannot even be addressed, let alone touched by changes in formal structures. Then there are some cases where there is so much micro-political interest involved in maintaining certain structural characteristics, that not even top management dares to attempt to change them.

In a process of organizational (re)design it is of essence to identify these immobile structural characteristics. To this end, regarding problems, one takes a look at the types of structures of an organization: can some programs be changed, and if yes, which ones? Can the existing communication channels be changed, and if yes, in which way? Which placements, transfers and redundancies of personnel are possible in order to influence the type of decisions at individual positions? On this basis, the chances for different change projects can be identified.

For instance, in the case of the world football federation, FIFA, it can be observed that there are ultimately very few possibilities remaining for reactions in regard to their multiple cases of corruption. In this sense, central decision premises at FIFA were immobilized. Simply put: a change in the upper echelons was out of the question for a long time, on account of the FIFA president's unwillingness to step down from his position following the revelation of corruption scandals, and the stability of his support network, which consisted of the presidents of smaller African, Asian and American countries. Changing conditional programs, such as restricting the participation of delegates who had already taken part in the FIFA congress twice, was in fact completely out of the question, as this would have significantly disturbed the existing networks. Ultimately, the only thing that could be done was a change in the communication channels in order to repair the federation's public image; an Independent Governance Committee was put in place whose role it was to process reform suggestions which, after adjustment, did not pose a threat to the core decision premises (FIFA 2012; for more on FIFA see Jennings 2006).

Even if every intervention depends on keeping an eye on the relation between the three structure types (programs, communication channels and personnel) and their manifestations in the display, formal and informal side, it could still be a mistake to try to simultaneously work on all structure types, in the sense of a "holistic approach." From a systems-theoretical point of view, there is an unrealistic management fantasy which underlies this holistic design aspiration. Niklas Luhmann (Luhmann 1964, 140) writes about how there is "probably only one unavoidable organizational law": not everything can be changed in the organization at the same time! The organization would end up dealing with more than it can handle if it tried to turn all the screws at the same time. It would run the risk of almost not recognizing itself anymore, and, in light of this danger, could even possibly end up in a state of shock induced paralysis.

3.4 On the Production of Variations in the Organization

When mobile structural characteristics are identified in an organization, it then becomes essential to develop variations for these structural characteristics which could be an attractive alternative for the organization. In classic change processes, organizations resort to the "Best Practice" of other organizations. This is potentially beneficial, as a suggestion for a new structure based on the success reports found in the display side of supposed "pioneer organizations" can seem very convincing. An organizational design based on systems-theory would very likely not forgo such a possibility. However, the variations would be derived from the specific "latencies" within the organization itself.

The idea behind it is that access to other—perhaps even more suitable—organizational structures can be found within those latencies. It is a matter of raising to the surface that which was previously inexistent and invisible due to structural decisions, and making it possible for employees to openly discuss. Precisely because organizations are always confronted by contradictory requirements and these contradictory requirements are partially hidden by structural decisions, there are possibilities to make visible what is hidden.

One possibility here is to bring to the foreground the dilemmas which are present in every organization by way of the existing constellations of conflict. With the term "dilemma" we refer to the difficulty in the face of two opposing alternatives, whenever equally good reasons for either can be found. In contrast to a paradox which cannot essentially be resolved, the concept of the dilemma applies more pressure on the organization to decide on one of the alternatives, however attractive the other approach may seem.

These dilemmas are usually hidden in the organizational practice. An initial strategy focusing on the technical dimension certainly consists of allowing the creation of local rationalities by setting up departments which are clearly separate from each other, yet also in attenuating the resulting conflicts by making excess resources available. Richard M. Cyert and James G. March (Cyert and March 1992, 41ff.) already indicated that goal conflicts in organizations that are hierarchical and structured in a strongly collaborative way can be reduced by assigning different organizational units to each one of the competing goals. The existing goal conflicts in the organization are interpreted as conflicts between the departments; conflicts which can nevertheless be reduced by sufficient organizational slack. In that way, excess financial resources can contribute to competing departments not having to reach mutual decisions. "In-between departments" reduce conflicts between production and sales divisions because not every disturbance necessarily affects the one or the other. As large, bureaucratically structured organizations are well able to deal with the organizational allocation of goal conflicts in different units and have resources at their disposal to attenuate the goal conflicts between the units, William H. Starbuck (Starbuck 1988, 67f.) considers them especially resilient to paradoxes.

A second strategy for the prevention of dilemmas, which focuses on the time dimension, consists in emphasizing only one side of the dilemma at a time, while at the same time leaving the option open of focusing on the other side of the dilemma at another time. From this point of view, one can read the history of several companies in the twentieth century as a permanent, wavelike shifting between two opposite poles. After a phase of diversification, the focus shifts to core competences, after which it goes back to diversification, so that it can then shift back to just a few core competences (Brunsson and Olsen 1993, 35ff.).

A third organizational strategy focusing on the social dimension consists in reformulating the dilemmas as problems of the members of the organization. Particularly in the training of manager roles—but increasingly of general employees as well—, fundamental contradictions in an organization are translated into personal dilemmas. A branch director must take and put under one roof the contradictory demands from higher management according to short-term profitability of their business area on the one hand, and long-term, the short-term profitability of weakening investments on the other. The head of production must find a way to reconcile the necessity of an undisturbed assembly line with a volatile market, as well as the innovative wishes of strategic management. To a certain degree, management can justify its existence by making dilemmas their own problem. If the conditions surrounding an organization were clear, the organization could simply appoint its mainframe computer as CEO and assign the middle management positions to the terminals attached to the mainframe (Luhmann 1964, 214).

When designing organizations, it is essential to allow dilemmas to be discussed through channels. The task of a company's management—but also that of public administrations, hospitals, churches or universities—consists more and more in sharpening the organization's perception for complexity by contributing to the unraveling of dilemmas. It is no longer a matter of understanding management as a unit which takes in all uncertainties and enables a value-generating technical core to function according to clear principles, as James D. Thompson (Thompson 1967, 10ff.) purports, but far more a matter of understanding management as an entity with the task of unraveling dilemmas.

In other words, we a are referring to a fundamentally different approach to conflicts that are caused by the contradictory requirements in an organization. The classic instrumental-rational view of conflicts is that they emerge from the opposition by a group of affected individuals to propositions that are reasonable for organizations and from the attempts to inform, persuade and—if all else fails—pressure the employees so they accept the necessity of the propositions. The concept of "resistance" is meant to suggest a rebellion by employees against the rational decisions of management, against the elaborate interventions of consultants or against the supposedly consensual decision of a group. It suggests that the opinions of the consultants, the decisions of management and the consensual position of the group provide the correct view of the organization's environment.

This narrowing of perspective is perhaps helpful when it comes to setting up a streamlined organization according to the point of view of management or consultants. However, in the case of establishing numerous perspectives, this supposedly rebellious attitude from employees can be understood as an attempt to put forth or maintain an additional perspective. It provides a wide range of operable materials for the design of organizations.

How then are selections made from the variations that result from the consulting process?

3.5 Promoting Selections

In the classic notion of organizational theory, it is assumed that at least one possible rational selection takes place between various alternative approaches. To make the best decision between all the different alternative approaches, the consequences of the different strategies should be analyzed and compared. Both in expert consulting as well as in organizational development, the elaborated structure of the organization is internally promoted with great marketing efforts. The employees are summoned to large conferences to be informed about the new structure. The new structure is depicted in staff magazines and PR campaigns are launched to promote the new measures.

An approach which is skeptical of instrumental rationality distances itself consistently from the notion that an ideal solution can be found for an organization in a design process. And how would it be possible to find an ideal solution for a situation in light of the contradictory goals of an organization? How could all the consequences of all the differently assessed alternatives be evaluated? How can one have any hope of making the ideal decision if it is not even possible to oversee all possible alternatives? In the ambiguous world of the organization—and as it has been made apparent by Karl Weick (Weick 1985, 352) et al.—decisions are either appropriate or inappropriate. The strategy which ultimately establishes itself is the result of organizational momentum, incidental market developments and a coincidental constellation of interests.

For that reason, in the framework of a process of organizational (re)design, it is often sensible to set, metaphorically speaking, not just one potentially successful train in the railway system of the organization, but to send off many at the same time and see how they perform. The different trains might dock next each other or cross each others paths, but they can also struggle for the same track or even crash. Unlike railway systems where it is essential to prevent trains from colliding, organizations are built in such a way that diverse and even contradictory strategies are allowed to be in operation at the same time (March 1981).

The ability of organizations to build organizational padding (slack) is utilized so that differing, competing strategies can be supplied with resources. The processes in organizations are often only loosely attached to each other, so that it is possible to deal with contradictions. Furthermore, the organization is able to function at a symbolic level, which allows it to contain the ambiguity and contradictions and not let them break out.

During the selection phase, it is the task of management and consultants to protect the different emerging and also contradictory concepts from the immune system of the organization. The resistance to new organizational structures which can be observed in a strong PR campaign for a measure should be avoided if possible. An effective method is the depiction of changes as "experiments," "tests" or "attempts". In this way, the impression is given that nothing is yet permanent as a consequence of the reorganization, and that everything is still open and reversible, depending on the results of these processes. In the end, the experiments and tests that establish themselves are the ones which cannot be avoided on a micro-political level, and which deliver a satisfying solution as soon as possible and for as many groups in the organization. Ultimately, it is a Darwinian process; the variations which are able to develop themselves in a niche of the organization are the ones that establish themselves and then spread out from there.

4. On Working with Latencies—Conclusion

One thing is important when working with latencies of organizations—it doesn't make sense to reveal all latencies in an organization during a design process. This would lead to a terrible neglect of the function of latencies. Ultimately, latencies protect the structure by dimming what is important yet shouldn't be seen. A manager who tries to completely understand all the problems of their employees, the market and technical processes would not quite embody the current model of the ideal "doer," but would instead be discriminated as a utopian "Organization Whisperer." Understandably, as Herbert A. Simon (Simon 1956, 129ff.) already pointed out, managers are not interested in knowing their organization inside out, but rather in making appropriate decisions.

A second view on the organization—the contemplation of latencies—presents a luxury which is not absolutely necessary in an organization (or in other systems). Without the first glance, one would be practically blind in the organization; management would not decide, employees would not produce, salespeople would not sell. Whether a second look makes sense depends on the circumstances; an observer can get blinded or disoriented if they project their own perspective against the reflective walls of a room. In a way, perspective is defined in how it allows us to see without it ever being visible as a "perspective."

For a management understanding based on systems-theory, it is therefore necessary to approach the latencies of an organization in two steps. The first step consists in determining which latencies are present in an organization. It is observed from an outside perspective which aspects are not (or only limitedly) detected. The point is to observe which dominant patterns were built by the organization for the construction of its reality; what differences are primarily used to operate; what can and cannot be seen with the help of these differences; which specific blind spots are generated; and which consequences come out as a result. As a second step it must also be determined whether the latent structures are so distinct that working on them would unsettle the whole organization, or if it would make sense to address these latencies.

Processing these latencies does not erase them from the face of the Earth. Rather, the point is to make them more manageable. Usually, the contradictory requirements hiding behind latencies cannot be wiped out by executive managers or consultants. It is only possible to find approaches which are more or less suitable for them.

Bibliography

Brunsson, Nils. 1989. *The Organization of Hypocrisy: Talk, Decisions and Actions in Organization*. Chichester: John Wiley.

Brunsson, Nils, and Johan P. Olsen. 1993. *The Reforming Organization*. New York: Routledge.

Cohen, Michael D., and James G. March and Johan P. Olsen. 1972. "A Garbage Can Model of Organizational Choice." *Administrative Science Quarterly*, no. 17: 1–25.

Cyert, Richard M., and March, James G. 1992. *A Behavioral Theory of the Firm*. Cambridge: Blackwell.

Dalton, Melville. 1959. *Men Who Manage*. New York: Wiley.

FIFA. 2012. *FIFA Governance Reform Project: First Report by the Independent Governance Comittee to the Executive Committee of FIFA*. Basel: FIFA.

Friedberg, Erhard. 1993. *Le pouvoir et la règle*. Paris: Seuil.

Jennings, Andrew. 2006. *FOUL! The Secret World of FIFA: Bribes, Vote-Rigging and Ticket Scandals*. London: HarperSport.

Kühl, Stefan. 2013. *Organizations: A Systems Approach*. Farnham: Gower.

Kühl, Stefan. 2018a (forthcoming). *Sisyphus in Management: The Futile Search for the Optimal Organizational Structure*. Princeton/Hamburg/Shanghai/Singapore/Versailles/Zurich: Organizational Dialogue Press.

Kühl, Stefan. 2018b (forthcoming). *The Rainmaker Effect: Contradictions of the Learning Organization*. Princeton/Hamburg/

Shanghai/Singapore/Versailles/Zurich: Organizational Dialogue Press.

Luhmann, Niklas. 1964. *Funktionen und Folgen formaler Organisation*. Berlin: Duncker & Humblot.

Luhmann, Niklas. 1973. *Zweckbegriff und Systemrationalität*. Frankfurt/M.: Suhrkamp.

Luhmann, Niklas. 1975. "Interaktion, Organisation, Gesellschaft." In *Soziologische Aufklärung 2*, published by Niklas Luhmann, 9–20. Opladen: WDV.

Luhmann, Niklas. 1995. *Social Systems*. Stanford: Stanford University Press.

Luhmann, Niklas. 2000. *Organisation und Entscheidung*. Opladen: WDV.

Luhmann, Niklas. 2006. "Communication Barriers in Management Consulting." In *Niklas Luhmann and Organization Studies*, published by Kai Helge Becker and David Seidl, 351–364. Philadelphia/Amsterdam: John Benjamins.

March, James G. 1981. "Footnotes to Organizational Change." *Administrative Science Quarterly*, no. 26: 563–577.

March, James G. 1990. "Anmerkungen zu organisatorischer Veränderung." In *Entscheidung und Organisation: Kritische und konstruktive Beiträge*, published by James G. March, 187–208. Wiesbaden: Gabler.

March, James G., and Herbert A. Simon. 1958. *Organizations*. New York: John Wiley.

Neuberger, Oswald. 1994. "Zur Ästhetisierung des Managements." In *Managementforschung 4*, published by Georg Schreyögg and Peter Conrad, 1–70. Berlin/New York: Walter de Gruyter.

Reemtsma, Jan Philipp. 2008. *Vertrauen und Gewalt: Versuch über eine besondere Konstellation der Moderne*. Hamburg: Hamburger Edition.

Rodríguez Mansilla, Darío. 1991. *Gestion organizacional: Elementos para su estudio*. Santiago de Chile: Pontificia Universidad Católica de Chile.

Simon, Herbert A. 1956. "Rational Choice and the Structure of the Environment." In *Psychological Review* 63: 129–138.

Simon, Herbert A. 1957. *Administrative Behavior*, 2nd ed. New York: The Free Press.

Starbuck, William H. 1988. "Surmounting Our Human Limitations." In *Paradox and Transformation: Toward a Theory of Change in Organization and Management*, published by Robert E. Quinn and Kim S. Cameron, 65–80. Cambridge: Ballinger.

Thompson, James D. 1967. *Organizations in Action*. New York: McGraw-Hill.

Weick, Karl E. 1979. *The Social Psychology of Organizing*. Reading: Addison-Wesley.

Weick, Karl E. 1985. *Der Prozeß des Organisierens*. Frankfurt a.M.: Suhrkamp.